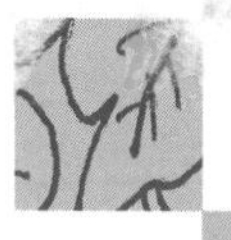

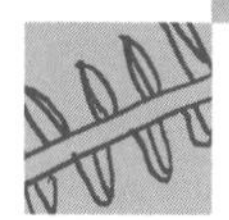

Reflections on Design Principles

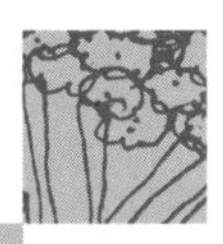

Emily Cousins

Expeditionary Learning
Outward Bound

KENDALL/HUNT PUBLISHING COMPANY
4050 Westmark Drive Dubuque, Iowa 52002

Expeditionary Learning℠ is a Service Mark of Outward Bound, Inc.
Outward Bound® is a Registered Trademark of Outward Bound, Inc.

ISBN 0-7872-4978-5

Printed in the United States of America
10 9 8 7 6 5 4 3 2 1

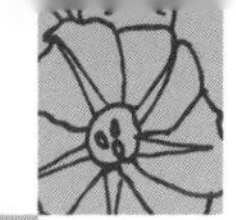
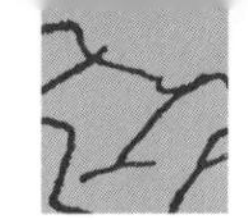
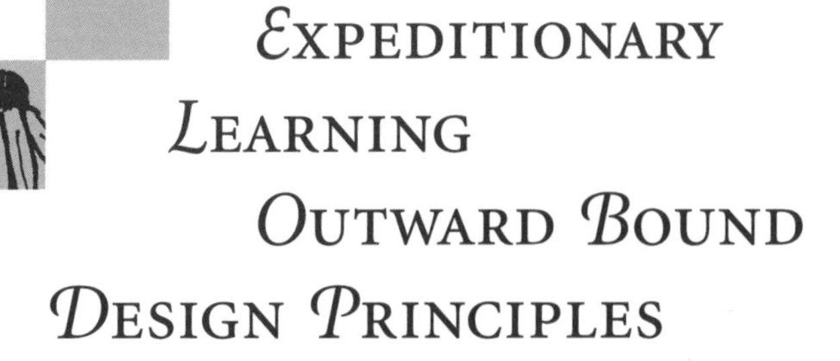

Expeditionary Learning Outward Bound Design Principles

The Primacy of Self-Discovery

The Having of Wonderful Ideas

The Responsibility for Learning

Intimacy and Caring

Success and Failure

Collaboration and Competition

Diversity and Inclusivity

The Natural World

Solitude and Reflection

Service and Compassion

Preamble to Design Principles

Learning is an expedition into the unknown. Expeditions draw together personal experience and intellectual growth to promote self-discovery and construct knowledge.

We believe that adults should guide students along this journey with care, compassion, and respect for their diverse learning styles, backgrounds, and needs.

ADDRESSING INDIVIDUAL DIFFERENCES PROFOUNDLY INCREASES THE POTENTIAL FOR LEARNING AND CREATIVITY OF EACH STUDENT.

GIVEN FUNDAMENTAL LEVELS OF HEALTH, SAFETY, AND LOVE, ALL PEOPLE CAN AND WANT TO LEARN. WE BELIEVE EXPEDITIONARY LEARNING HARNESSES THE NATURAL PASSION TO LEARN AND IS A POWERFUL METHOD FOR DEVELOPING THE CURIOSITY, SKILLS, KNOWLEDGE, AND COURAGE NEEDED TO IMAGINE A BETTER WORLD AND WORK TOWARD REALIZING IT.

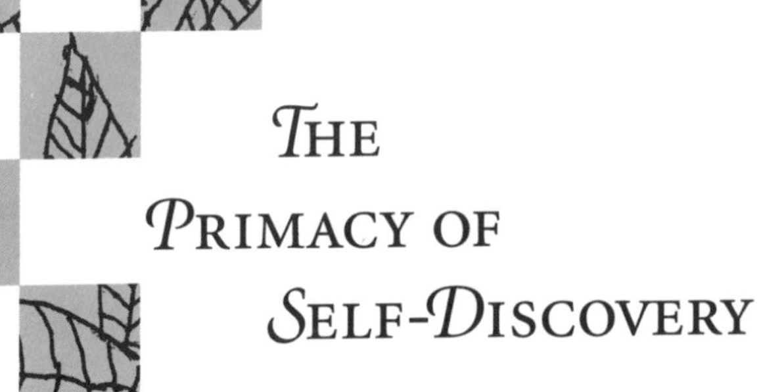

The Primacy of Self-Discovery

Know thyself.

—Socrates

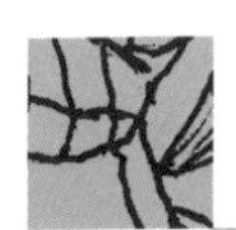

Caminante, no hay camino,
se hace el camino al andar.

Walker, there is no road,
you must make your own road
as you go.

—Antonio Machado

Learning happens best with emotion, challenge, and the requisite support.

People discover their abilities, values, "grand passions," and responsibilities in situations that offer adventure and the unexpected.

They must have tasks that require perseverance, fitness, craftsmanship, imagination, self-discipline, and significant achievement.

A primary job of the educator is to help students overcome their fear and discover they have more in them than they think.

Throughout the centuries and across cultures, literature, religion, mythology, and philosophy exhort us to know ourselves, and to plumb the depths of human motivations, yearnings, and actions. From Socrates to Buddha, wise people tell us that self-knowledge makes life richer and more fulfilling. Expeditionary Learning schools take to heart this wisdom of the ages. Students learn far more than mere facts and figures. They discover who they are as individuals, as members of a community, and as learners. Adventure helps them find unknown strengths, and service fosters a sense of commitment to others. The variety of project work in Expeditionary Learning classrooms nurtures untapped talents and stirs new passions for learning. Perhaps most importantly, the challenges of Expeditionary Learning help students stretch past perceived limits and discover that they have more in them than they thought.

Experiences that engage the emotions generate self-discovery. "Our feelings are our most genuine paths to knowledge," observes writer and activist Audre Lorde. "They are chaotic, sometimes painful, sometimes contradictory, but they come from deep within us. And we must key into those feelings.... This is how new visions begin."[1] The thrill of rappelling into a canyon or the sadness evoked by reading Toni Morrison's *Beloved* can awaken curiosity and understanding students did not know they had. When students discover an idea that moves or excites them, they are inspired to research, reflect, and learn more.

These emotional triggers often reveal passionate interests. Expeditionary Learning places great value on pursuing passions, because we believe it encourages students to be lifelong, engaged learners. Loretta Brady, a teacher at School for the Physical City in New York City, explains that "Outward Bound reminds us that you have to help young people uncover their passions—not just learning styles, but passions. If through their work they start to discover that inner fire, then they are better able to see the possibilities for making an impact in the world."[2] The more students engage deeply with—the more novels they read, physics problems they tackle, artists they meet, community activists they interview—the more they will find to be passionate about. Intense exploration launches countless investigations, for as Voltaire wrote, "The passions are the winds that fill the sails of a vessel."

Adventure and the unexpected stir evocative responses and help students discover new passions and talents. For instance, teachers who attend the Civil Rights Summit in Memphis, Tennessee—a week-long professional development experience for teachers modeled on learning expeditions[3]—develop unexpected talents when they plunge into new experiences. A biology teacher discovers an interest in writing poetry after she writes about fieldwork in the Mississippi Delta. Another teacher decides he likes to perform after he and his colleagues dramatize a lunch counter sit-in for an audience at the Civil Rights Museum in Memphis. The wide range of activities in summits, Outward Bound courses, and learning expeditions often provides each individual with an opportunity to make new discoveries.

Steven Levy, a fourth-grade teacher in Lexington, Massachusetts, creates a sense of adventure right in his classroom by challenging his students to complete seemingly impossible tasks. "I always want my students to feel that it can't be done. And then somehow, we do it," he explains.[4] One summer he emptied his classroom, and when the students arrived in September, he suggested that they design and furnish the room themselves. He reminded the students that, like the Pilgrims they would be studying throughout the year, they needed to rely on limited resources and their own ingenuity. As the students grappled with the first steps of acquiring and storing pencils, the idea of building furniture appeared insurmountable. They turned to Pilgrim diaries for inspiration, and slowly, with each step of talking with carpenters and calculating the amount of supplies, the challenging goals became attainable. The varied nature of research and construction offered students many ways to discover unknown talents.

Facing unfamiliar challenges can inspire fear, but with the appropriate support, students and teachers can persevere and succeed. When Dubuque teacher Fran Kennedy found herself climbing through a cave for a professional development summit on geology, she thought she would never make it. "Inside the cave," she remembers, "when the cold damp boulders pushed in on me, when the darkness was illumi-

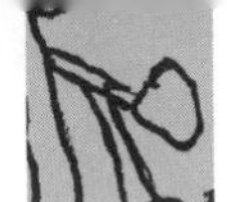

nated only by a flashlight strapped to my helmet, and when the next step was an eight-foot drop, I thought, 'I can't do this.' But I did. I'm glad I did. I learned to take a risk, to accept help, to seize opportunities, and to be responsible for my own learning."[5]

As so many writers, artists, and philosophers have reminded us, the road to self-discovery is riddled with challenges and pitfalls. Yet just as important as discovering a passion is facing the challenges necessary to sustain and expand it. With greater self-knowledge and more perseverance, students will cultivate new interests and surpass standards they did not know they could reach.

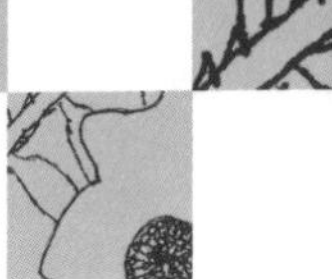

The Having of Wonderful Ideas

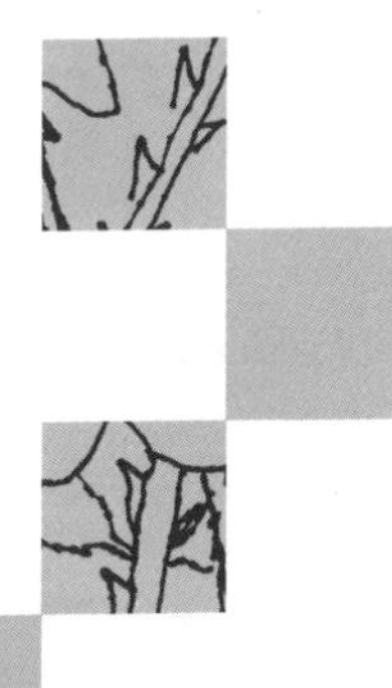

Exhaust the little moment.

—Gwendolyn Brooks

The Possible's slow fuse is lit
By the Imagination.

—Emily Dickinson

Once you wake up thought in a man,
you can never put it to sleep again.

—Zora Neale Hurston

Teach so as to build on children's curiosity about the world by creating learning situations that provide matter to think about, time to experiment, and time to make sense of what is observed.

Foster a community where students' and adults' ideas are respected.

In the midst of a class discussion, a sophomore's hand shoots up into the air with an insight she cannot wait to share. After pondering a math problem, a second grader begins to squirm in his seat with the anticipation of sharing his answer. These images capture the burst of energy that comes when a student has a wonderful idea. According to Eleanor Duckworth, a professor at the Harvard Graduate School of Education, wonderful ideas are those ideas that children create for themselves based on their own knowledge and curiosity. Often the right question asked at the right time will inspire students to invent wonderful ideas. If the children are engaged, they will tax themselves to construct the ideas that form a good answer. These ideas, Duckworth believes, are the stepping stones of intellectual development. Not only do they further content knowledge, but they also cultivate habits of inquiry, exploration, and self-confidence.

"The mind is not a vessel to be filled, but a fire to be lighted," wrote Plutarch. Like fires, wonderful ideas need fuel to ignite them. "Intelligence cannot develop without matter to think about," Duckworth observes. "Making new connections depends on knowing enough about something in the first place to provide a basis for thinking of other things to do—of other questions to ask—that demand more complex connections in order to make sense."[6] Rich learning environments provide the raw material that suggest wonderful ideas to children.

For example, students at Deering High School in Portland, Maine, started their learning expedition on location by examining fundamental concepts in physics, pre-calculus, and computer science. With that background, they embarked on group projects. One group began by tinkering with a solenoid, an electrical-mechanical motor, that teacher Jon Sweeney had placed in the lab. Their knowledge of flux density and magnetic fields brought them to a certain level in grasping the solenoid, but when Sweeney made a comment about crossing the vector of a current, their next foothold of understanding seemed just out of reach. Sweeney declined to offer more information, so it was up to the students to bridge the distance.

The students began experimenting with the solenoid, and, as one student explains, they reached a plateau in their work. "Then, rather suddenly, we realized that we could measure the strength of the force by putting small weights on the opposite side of the board from where the current was running. We shared this idea with Mr. Sweeney and sure enough he told us that's exactly how it works."[7] With the combination of their background knowledge and their experimentation, they jumped to a deeper level of understanding.

Such learning experiences require that teachers and students value the unexpected. Children may have wonderful ideas at any time during the school day, and that might mean that planned activities have to be postponed because a child's thought process leads the class down an unanticipated avenue.

During a learning expedition on frogs, for instance, a first grader at Lincoln School in Dubuque, Iowa, came in from recess and recited a poem about frogs she had just made up. The class enjoyed it so much that teacher Lorie Duclos changed her plans for the afternoon so everyone could write frog poems. Duclos says that in the past she might have asked the student to put the poem in her portfolio and returned to her lesson plan. Her experience with Expeditionary Learning, though, inspired her to do something different. "This time I took her motivation and everybody else's excitement in hearing her poem as a whole learning experience."[8]

In this type of classroom, the role of the teacher shifts from lecturer to guide. The teacher remains alert to the intellectual possibilities of the topic at hand, but she does not hastily supply directions or answers. Instead, she allows the students to pursue their own ideas. "We'd never say, 'You ought to quit this and go this way,'" explained the Deering teachers. "Instead, we'd ask a question. For instance, 'Is there any way you can control the strength of this magnetic field with your apparatus?' We felt that if they tackled questions like that, they'd come up with their own answers."[9]

Respect for students is at the base of any classroom that supports the having of wonderful ideas. Building such a classroom begins with accepting that children will do things many different ways, and that there is not simply one Wonderful Idea. When teachers honor those ideas as they emerge,

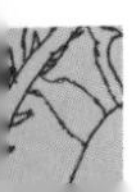

students begin to feel more confident in exploring uncharted territory. A Deering teacher remarked, "The main difference between these students and those in other, more conventional classes we've taught is that they are what we call brave learners. They're not afraid to step into a situation they're unfamiliar with.... They take [the material] apart and put it back together in so many ways that they seem to understand it far better than any group we've worked with before."[10]

Expeditionary Learning schools encourage all students to posit, question, and explore instead of simply repeat and fill in the blanks. The students have time and space to pursue spontaneous inspirations. They learn to think.

The Responsibility for Learning

I become more courageous
by doing the very things I
needed to be courageous for—first, a little,
and badly. Then, bit by bit, more and better.
Being avidly—sometimes annoyingly—
curious and persistent about discovering
how others were doing what I wanted to do.

—Audre Lorde

What is an Expeditionary Learning School?
A school where you try to find things
out for yourself. The teacher doesn't
just tell you.

—Second Grader, Dubuque, Iowa

Learning is both a personal, individually specific process of discovery and a social activity.

Each of us learns within and for ourselves and as a part of a group.

Every aspect of a school must encourage children, young people, and adults to become increasingly responsible for directing their own personal and collective learning.

Many Native American cultures believe that when young people want to learn a traditional craft, they must learn by doing it themselves. If Lummi girls want to weave baskets or Yurok boys want to make bows, they find an elder who knows the craft, and they carefully watch him or her doing it. The elder does not lecture or explain each detail, for that would rob the young people of their learning experience and leave them without a way to think for themselves when the elder is gone. Instead, the elder models the craft until the children feel confident enough to try it for themselves. The children might make many mistakes along the way, but once they create a well-made form, they will never forget how to do it, for they have mastered the craft through their own actions and learning.

Expeditionary Learning schools pass on the craft of learning in a similar manner. Teachers model the process of ongoing inquiry and offer support, but the students construct their own knowledge. Since there are no simple, fill-in-the-blank answers in complex project work, students must solve problems themselves and reach their own conclusions. They become the fuel for their learning, as opposed to relying on the momentum of a teacher. Through this process, students learn far more than a set amount of material; they learn how to learn—a habit of mind they will never forget, because they have established it through their own experience.

As students take responsibility for their learning, the role of the teacher changes. No longer

do they have to appear to know everything. Rather they, like their students, can be learners. They explore, reflect, revise, and consult colleagues to tackle problems. Expeditionary Learning Outward Bound professional development opportunities foster a sense of inquiry and encourage teachers to take risks. "The message I received [at the Geology Summit] was that it was all right not to know all the answers," explains Vivian Stephens, a fourth-grade teacher at Clairemont Elementary School in Decatur, Georgia. "If I had had to know everything before taking the first step in teaching this expedition, I would never have undertaken it." Not only is this realization liberating for a teacher, but it also provides students with an essential model of the learning process. Now, when Stephens' students ask her something she does not know, she can say, "I don't know. Let's go find out," or "I'm learning like you."[11] As another Expeditionary Learning teacher observed, "Each expedition offers me an opportunity to learn. That is an important quality for my students to see."

In the context of shared learning, the teacher's role shifts from teacher as purveyor of knowledge to teacher as guide. Teachers instruct students in the skills they need to meet outcomes and standards, but they do not supply all the answers nor dictate the route students must take. Taking the step back can be challenging for teachers. "What usually happens in these situations is that teachers say we're going to let them do it on their own but then we end up doing it for them," says Mary Lynn Lewark, a former teacher at Rocky Mountain School of Expeditionary Learning in Denver, Colorado. To prevent this, Lewark says, "I'm always asking myself, 'Am I doing something that my students could be doing for themselves?'"[12]

Encouraging students to steer their own learning does not free them from high expectations. Clearly articulated standards point students toward excellence. In traditional schools, students are not aware of the standards by which they are evaluated. Assessment often takes place in silent testing rooms, while the answer sheet or grading rubric remains locked in the teacher's desk. In Expeditionary Learning schools, teachers and students discuss standards on a daily basis so students fully understand what constitutes quality work. Together they list the components of a well-written book review, the steps in a solid scientific experiment, or the elements of an accurate architectural drawing. When Karen McDonald at King Middle School in Portland, Maine, leads her "Facing Issues" learning expedition, she shows students exemplary work from past years. The well-crafted brochures about drug dependency, homelessness, and racism show students exactly how other students achieved high quality work. With clear expectations and McDonald's support, the students become the agents of their own success.

When students begin to feel a sense of responsibility for their endeavors, they also feel a greater sense of investment and pride. Students rarely get excited about presenting a report when their

teacher tells them what to write. But when students discover answers for themselves and create their own products, they become engaged and eager to share them with a larger audience. When Kathy Greeley's eighth-grade class at Graham and Parks School in Cambridge, Massachusetts, took on the responsibility of creating and producing a play about social action, they became deeply invested in the play's success. After the production met with resounding praise, one student wrote to her teacher: "I felt proud. I felt more pride than I'd felt for almost anything in my whole life. I was proud of myself, I was proud of you, but most of all I was proud of the class as a whole. It was amazing to realize what a great thing we could create by working together."[13] A sense of achievement is most profound and lasting when students know that they themselves are responsible for creating it.

Intimacy and Caring

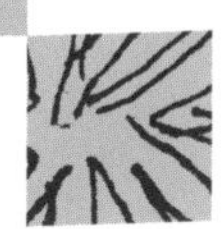

And there at the camp
we had around us the
elemental world of
water and light and earth and air. We felt the
presences of the wild creatures, the river, the
trees, the stars.

Though we had our troubles,
we had them in true perspective. The
universe, as we could see any night, is
unimaginably large, and mostly dark.
We knew we needed to be together more
than we needed to be apart.

—Wendell Berry

Learning is fostered best in small groups where there is trust, sustained caring, and mutual respect among all members of the learning community.

Keep schools and learning groups small.

Be sure there is a caring adult looking after the progress of each child. Arrange for the older students to mentor the younger ones.

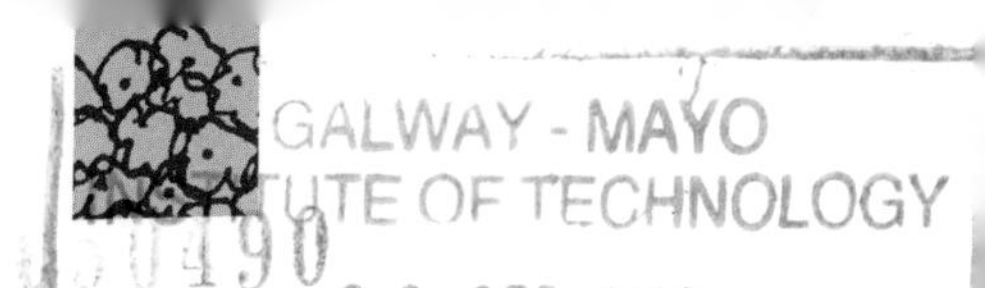

Most Italian towns center around a piazza where people stroll in the evenings and visit at outdoor cafés. Plains Indian teepee encampments circle around a central point in which tribal members hold feasts, honor community members, or dance. Both of these cultures have a "city" plan that responds to the human need to gather and be a part of a whole. Both seem to realize that people come together when a place is inviting, safe, and at the center of things. Expeditionary Learning recognizes the importance of giving community a space in which to grow. In Expeditionary Learning schools, community circles and small groups build the physical space, while communication, respect, and compassion create the emotional and intellectual space of a classroom community. Like the piazza, the classroom becomes a welcoming environment, for this communal space is built on the principles of intimacy and caring.

Expeditionary Learning focuses on the architecture of community because we believe that learning happens best in an atmosphere of trust and sustained caring. Not only do such communities nurture students' sense of self-confidence and ability, they also teach the skills students need to become active members of a respectful society. Kurt Hahn, the founder of Outward Bound, believed strongly in the relationship between individual and communal growth. Drawing from Plato's *Republic*, he asserted that a person could not reach perfection without becoming a part of a perfect society. Indeed, personal development is of questionable value if it is not

linked to communal development. Compassion, Hahn believed, was the value that would remind students to strive for the well-being of others as well as for their own success. Expeditionary Learning schools try to strike a similar balance. Students are encouraged to participate in a reciprocal relationship with the school community. They draw strength from the group's support and, in return, they give a sense of respect and compassion to their fellow community members.

These relationships are challenging to build. Expeditionary Learning schools have found that daily community circles are an excellent way to begin. Community circles allow the whole class to reflect on the day and talk about concerns in the classroom. To insure that students feel comfortable expressing their feelings and ideas, most classes agree upon appropriate conduct. Shari Flatt, a teacher at Table Mound Elementary School in Dubuque, Iowa, says she and her first graders have certain rules for circle: "We have to hold still, our eyes are on the speaker, and we are quiet. All of those things add up to being a good listener. We just keep practicing them over and over again."[14] Through practice, students create an environment in which individuals are treated with sensitivity and respect. "What we build together in our community circle is felt throughout the day," says Tammy Duehr, Shari Flatt's colleague. "They can speak directly to one another through the circle, and they know they can do it in a safe way."[15]

Like community circles, small groups help foster that sense of safety and closeness. When farmer

Wes Jackson was asked why he only accepted ten or twelve students in his sustainable agricultural school he answered, "I decided a long time ago not to have more students than can fit around a campfire."[16] The image of the campfire conveys the warmth, ease, support, and camaraderie that can emerge among small groups. Small groups cover more ground than large, unwieldy ones, and they learn how to draw on individual strengths to succeed. This idea of campfire-sized groups may seem foreign to big urban schools, but Expeditionary Learning schools have discovered ways to create intimacy in the face of a large class size. Teaching teams encourage their students to work in collaborative groups on expedition projects. In some schools, small groups conduct fieldwork with one of the teachers and parent volunteers, while the rest of the class does research at school.

At Pathfinder School in Seattle, Washington, teacher Chris Weaver split his second- and third-grade class into two groups, the Tortoises and the Sea Turtles. Each afternoon, one group met for a daily meeting, while the other group quietly wrote in their journals. "The journal writers did in fact remain silent, because they were listening to the voices of their classmates expressing and solving problems, usually with some humor and some drama," Weaver observed. "The two groups became like bands and held their shape."[17]

Over time, community circles and small group work create a safety net over which students feel safe taking intellectual, emotional, and physical

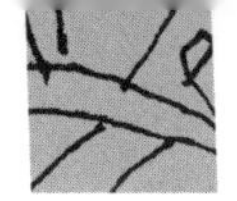

risks in the company of their peers. When Vivian Stephens, a teacher at Clairemont Elementary School in Decatur, Georgia, presented her class with three different options for mastering reading skills, she was surprised when they chose to use peer mentors. "I think they chose this approach because they had started trusting each other so that nobody was afraid to show his or her weaknesses and ask for help," says Stephens. "That moment was a beautiful outgrowth of the team building we'd been doing."[18]

While it is essential that students forge strong ties with fellow students, it is also important for them to become close with adults in the school community. Multiyear teaching, in which teachers remain with the same class for at least two years, provides an opportunity for students and teachers to get to know each other over time. "In my past experience it would have taken me at least three months to get to know my students and develop a relationship with them," explains Magda Rodriguez, a teacher at Rafael Hernandez School in Boston, Massachusetts, who followed her second graders into third. "Whereas this fall they knew me and I knew them. They knew the class rules and my teaching styles, and I knew what they needed to progress."[19] The classroom as a whole benefits from the continuity, familiarity, and deepened sense of community.

Expeditionary Learning classrooms encourage students and teachers to focus on building trust and respect among themselves. Yet this vision of community does not end with the small group in a single classroom. Students do not form communities so that they can shut themselves off from others. Rather, Expeditionary Learning communities face out to the larger world. Students bring the confidence, caring, and sensitivity they learn in the classroom out into the communities of the school, neighborhood, town, country, and globe. And as Hahn understood, both the students and the communities benefit.

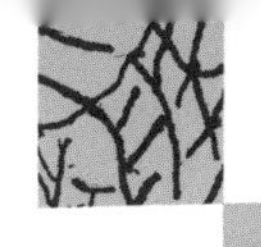

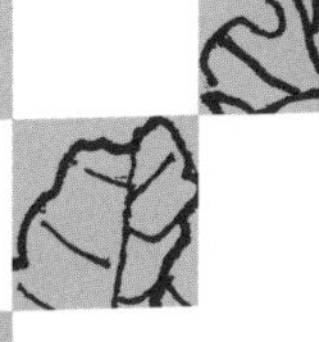

Success and Failure

Your disability
is your opportunity.

—Kurt Hahn

All my work is meant to say,
"You may encounter defeats,
but you must not be defeated."

—Maya Angelou

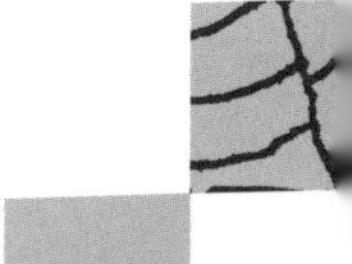

If there is no struggle, there is no progress.
Those who profess to favor freedom, and to
depreciate agitation, are those
who want crops without
plowing up the ground.

—Frederick Douglass

All students must be assured a fair measure of success in learning in order to nurture the confidence and capacity to take risks and rise to increasingly difficult challenges.

But it is also important to experience failure, to overcome negative inclinations, to prevail against adversity, and to learn to turn disabilities into opportunities.

On a small stream in Western Massachusetts, a group of teachers busied themselves with measuring tape, meter sticks, and surveying equipment. They were collecting data on water flow and stream dynamics for the Rocks, Rivers, and Caves Summit—a week-long learning expedition for educators on geology. After working hard all day, they were stunned when the geologists who were leading the summit told them their findings were invalid. Measurements had not been standardized, teams had overlapped without communicating, and common reference points had not been established. When the teachers realized the degree of mistakes, they were discouraged. But, as summit leader Ron Berger said, "The day was anything but a waste." Those first mistakes gave them the tools to succeed during the next day of research.

After carefully discussing procedures for the next day, the teachers were ready to give it another try. Groups repeatedly consulted with one another, systems of organization were clarified, and those teachers who had been unconcerned with exact measurement the day before became sticklers about measurement standards. "None of this organization came from me," remarked Berger. "On the contrary, I was criticized at one point for calling out time intervals too irregularly. The team, the group, forged our precision."[20] Through the failures of the first day, the teachers had learned what it would take to succeed the next time around.

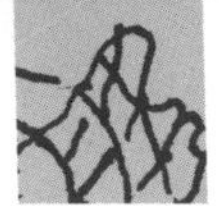

Kurt Hahn appreciated the close interrelationship between success and failure. At Gordonstoun, the secondary school Hahn started in Scotland, students had opportunities to succeed in academics, service, athletics, and leadership. Yet success without the experience of some level of failure, he believed, brought only a limited sense of accomplishment. Hahn "valued mastery in the sphere of one's weakness over performance in the sphere of one's strength."[21] At Gordonstoun, for instance, outstanding scholars were encouraged to work hard on the athletic field, while gifted athletes were encouraged to progress in academics. After experiencing a few inevitable setbacks, students who succeed in the face of obstacles make the greatest strides in their learning.

Expeditionary Learning classrooms nurture perseverance. They offer all students the chance to experience a certain level of success, thus building the confidence necessary to risk failure. The project work of learning expeditions offers different students the opportunity to succeed in different ways. For example, on a North Carolina Outward Bound wilderness course for educators, Amy Mednick of Expeditionary Learning felt she had failed herself when, on her solo, she sought help from her instructors during a storm. Her crew mates assured her that she was successful in getting the support she needed to make it through her solo. "It was like climbing that rockface," said Janet Weingartner, principal of Midway School in Cincinnati, Ohio. "When you couldn't move forward,

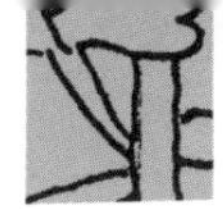

you moved laterally, and then started up again. It's the same with our children."[22]

In order for students to extend themselves beyond the safety of their successes, however, they must believe that if they fail along the way, they will be neither ridiculed nor rebuked. They need to have trust in their peers and teachers, as well as in themselves. This trust is built over time by fostering a sense of respect and support within the classroom community. The teachers on the geology summit, for instance, had already helped one another through the physically and emotionally challenging experience of cave exploration when they started their work on the stream. Knowing they could count on each other, they were willing to face the difficulties of revising their research.

Letting the tension of success and failure run its course can be challenging for the teacher as well as for the student. It can be tempting to intervene when a student is obviously headed down a bumpy road. When Ron Berger watched from the bank of the stream as teachers bungled their measurements, it was hard for him not to shout teacherly advice from the sidelines: "Do it this way....Start here....That won't work....Set yourselves up at regular intervals." He refrained because he knew that the teachers' missteps were essential to their learning. Because the teachers had experienced for themselves why and how they needed to do their research differently, they were able to bring their work to a more sophisticated level. In

fact, John Reid, a professor of Geology at Hampshire College in Amherst, Massachusetts, and co-leader of the summit, said he would like to use the teachers' findings as a basis for a professional paper. As Ron Berger said, "Suddenly that wasted day did not seem so wasted after all."[23]

Collaboration and Competition

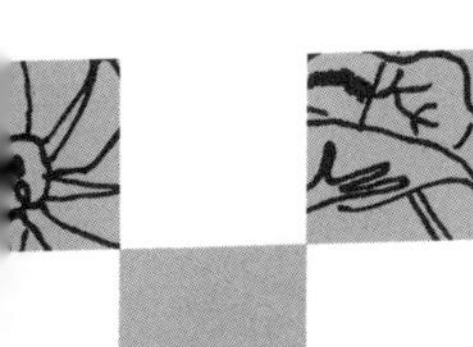

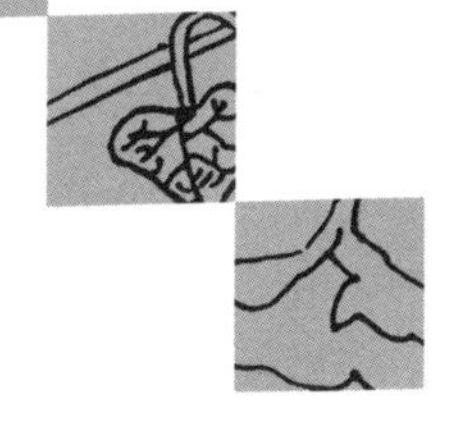

By mutual confidence and mutual aid
great deeds are done, and
great discoveries made.

—Homer

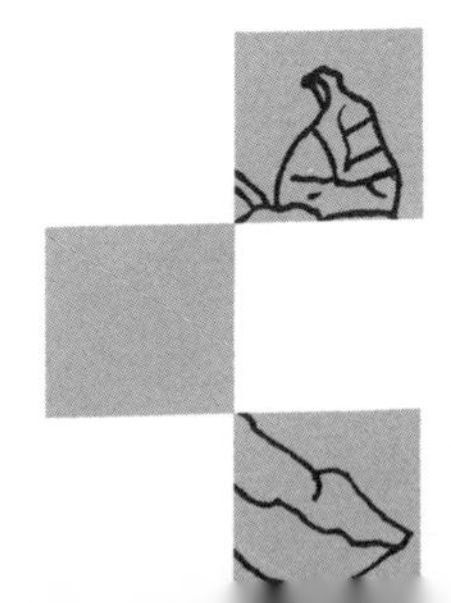

Teach so as to join individual and group development so that the value of friendship, trust, and group endeavor is made manifest.

Encourage students to compete, not against each other, but with their own personal best and with rigorous standards of excellence.

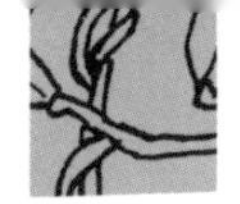

In a mainstream culture that celebrates the lone cowboy and the ambitious entrepreneur, Expeditionary Learning offers alternative methods for achieving success. Rather than going it alone, students turn to their peers for help in completing a task. Instead of trying to outsmart their colleagues, students compete with their own personal best to achieve higher goals. More collaboration and less competition raises the level of learning throughout the classroom, since students are contributing to the success of group projects as well as striving to meet individual challenges. Striking this balance, however, can only be done in an atmosphere of mutual respect and friendship. Educational philosopher Maxine Greene points out that friendship, as Aristotle saw it, was "a way of getting pleasure from another's achievements, celebrating what another authentically chooses."[24] In such a relationship, students focus not on thwarting their peers' success, but on contributing to it. In turn, each student has the support needed to surpass his or her previous accomplishments.

When a doctor confronts a complicated case, she does not shut herself behind closed doors to solve the problem. She enlists the help of other specialists. Similarly, architects, politicians, farmers, social workers, and countless other professionals draw from the expertise of their colleagues when they face challenges. Although it may be common in schools, it is rare in working life that professionals have to take tests without being allowed to consult peers seated right next to them. In an effort to break down the

walls between classroom and real-world standards, Expeditionary Learning schools cultivate the habits of professional collaboration within the school community.

In addition to individual work, small group cooperative projects are at the heart of learning expeditions. By their very nature, these projects call for collaboration. To complete them, students must discuss goals, divide responsibilities, and draw on each other's strengths. For instance, when students at School for the Physical City in New York City traveled to the Mission Society's camp in upstate New York to design cabins for the Society to build, the students had to work together. Each group had to come to consensus about the layout of the cabins, the building pattern, and whether or not the cabins should be built near local wetlands. Some students were able to help their group mates draw architectural plans to scale; others collaborated on assessing environmental impact. This level of cooperation did not always come easily. "Working in groups was hard," observed one of the students. "We had to make a lot of decisions, and there were a lot of arguments, but we had to complete something."[25] Despite the difficulties, the students came to place the group's success above individual interests or gains. In the process, they learned how to negotiate, debate, assist, and be responsible to their peers.

Like their students, teachers also benefit from opportunities to collaborate with one another. The culture of teachers working alone behind the closed doors of their classrooms has left many educators feeling isolated. But most Expeditionary Learning teachers guide learning expeditions in teams. This not only helps teachers learn from one another's expertise and resources, but allows them to model skills for students. As one high school teacher commented, "We are asking these young people to be interdisciplinary....How could we possibly model interdisciplinary learning if we didn't practice it ourselves?"[26] But the spirit of collaboration does not end with teaming. At Newberry Elementary School in Memphis, Tennessee, and Hyde Park Elementary School in Cincinnati, Ohio, teachers visit each other's classrooms to learn from their colleagues' instructional practices. In San Antonio, Texas, teachers from three Expeditionary Learning elementary schools are working together on an original research project examining how project-based learning can promote literacy development. In Expeditionary Learning schools across the country, more and more teachers are turning to their colleagues for support and professional growth.

It may seem that the principle of competition is out of place in a community that fosters collaboration. Indeed, when competition is turned against one's peers, it can be destructive and alienating. As John Ruskin wrote, "Nothing is ever done beautifully which is done in rivalship; or nobly, which is done in pride." However, when the challenge of competition is channeled toward surpassing one's own personal best, competition can be a positive and inspiring

force. Kurt Hahn believed that physical activity—traditionally riddled with rivalry—could demonstrate the process of striving for personal discipline and success. At Gordonstoun, students developed individual training plans and set daily goals for their progress in physical activities. Each student competed with himself and his own self-perceived limits. Slowly, these physical activities became far more than mere exercises; they became an instrument for "training the will for mastery."

Students can compete against an intellectual best in the same way they strive for a physical best. For instance, Ron Berger, a sixth-grade teacher in Shutesbury, Massachusetts, simply tells his class, "Your best work is what's required of you." Instead of making an "A" student complacent or a "C" student stop trying, Berger's classroom culture demands that every student reach for his or her own best achievement. "The grading system in my classroom is, it's 'A+' or it's not finished," Berger says. "If it's not their best work, it's not acceptable. And things just go back and back for revision." Clearly articulated standards, peer critique sessions, sustained collaboration, and constant revision help students reach this challenge. Students come to realize that revising work does not mean they "got it wrong." It just means they could continue to improve it. "In fact," Berger says, "some students develop a perverse pride. If you visited my class they'd say, 'I did fifteen drafts of this.' The status

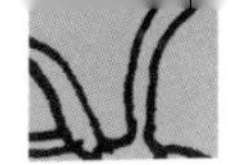

is switched from 'who got it right the first time' to 'who took the most care with it.'"[27]

Taking care is perhaps one of the most important values behind the principle of Collaboration and Competition. When students take care with their work, they defy low expectations and challenge themselves to do their best. When they take care with their responsibilities to team members, they create an antidote to isolation and selfishness. They discover the bonds of shared commitment that strengthen the school community.

Diversity and Inclusivity

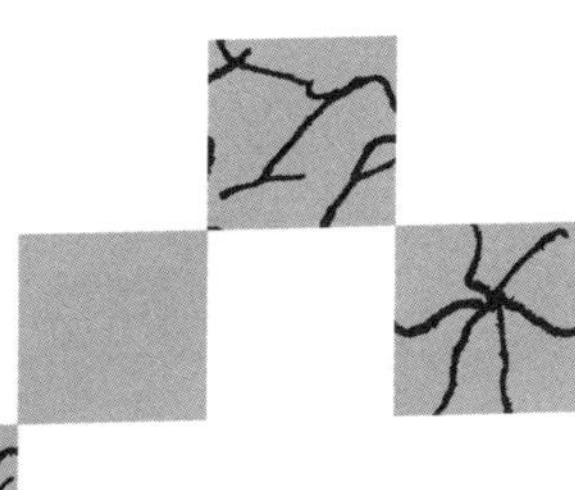

A person is a person because he recognizes others as persons.

—Desmond Tutu

Men who know the same things are not long the best company for each other.

—Emerson

Diversity and inclusivity in all groups dramatically increases richness of ideas, creative power, problem-solving ability, and acceptance of others.

Encourage students to investigate, value, and draw upon their own different histories, talents, and resources together with those of other communities and cultures. Keep the school and learning groups heterogeneous.

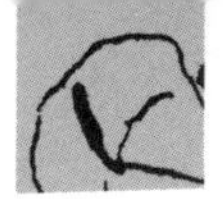

Some people may think that the call for diversity and inclusivity is a political abstraction. Yet as any student of the natural environment knows, the benefits of diversity are written all over the landscape. In the mixed-grass prairies of Southern Iowa, diversity is the key to life. Scores of prairie grasses and leafy plants establish relationships with one another that help maintain the ecosystem's balance. In contrast, when one weed chokes out other plants or a single crop repeatedly dominates the same ground, the land begins to lose its health. Monoculture crops cannot put down deep roots, causing tons of soil to blow away in the wind. Since single crops do not release enough nutrients into the ground, farmers often have to rely on chemical fertilizers. In essence, the lack of variety thwarts the creativity of the land.

Expeditionary Learning asserts that similar forces are at play in human cultures. Communities in which everyone has the same opinions, talents, and backgrounds may find it hard to generate new ideas or accept change. These monocultures become especially destructive when they exclude people based on ability, race, or class. Not only does this perpetuate injustice, but it also breeds a fear of difference. Expeditionary Learning believes that diversity fosters learning. Students develop knowledge and character through challenge, debate, and exchange, not through constant assent. They grow by learning about a number of traditions, not by drawing from one cultural norm. Expeditionary Learning schools strive to mix students in heterogeneous groups. All students are

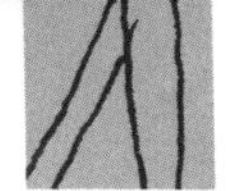

honored for what they bring to the community and all are encouraged to succeed.

The first step to building an inclusive learning community is realizing that there are many routes to knowledge. In the fields of literature and mathematics, scholars recognize that there are countless ways to interpret a poem and different algorithms for the same operation. Similarly, a visual learner might learn to read by recognizing words, while a kinesthetic learner might learn by copying sentences out of a book. Both students learn to read in the end. Too often, schools assume that there is only one way to arrive at a correct answer. Yet, as Harvard Professor Eleanor Duckworth points out, a variety of approaches enriches the classroom community. "In many cases if a child does something other than what you expected, it's not 'No,' it is another 'Yes.' The more different yes's we have in a classroom, the more everybody learns."[28]

Learning expeditions foster this type of richness. Since their multi-faceted projects appeal to different intelligences, learning expeditions include and challenge students with a wide variety of learning styles. In a high school math expedition at Rocky Mountain School of Expeditionary Learning in Denver, Colorado, for instance, the students had to design a water fountain, chart the height and width of the water arc, and find the arc's quadratic equations, angles, and water speed. While all the students were accountable for the same project, there was room to excel in different areas.Those who struggled with the precision of quadratic equations could demonstrate their conceptual understanding through journal writing. Those who had trouble creating artful designs could dive into the construction of the class fountain.

In many schools, these students might have been segregated into ability groups because of their different strengths. Not only does this make limiting assumptions about students' potential, but it can also make students believe they will never succeed in a high-ranked class. In Expeditionary Learning schools, all students are expected to reach high standards. Some need highly individualized learning contracts; some need support for severe physical or intellectual challenges. But they receive this assistance side-by-side all the other students. The flexibility of the learning expedition makes this possible. Since teachers do not have to keep students on the same page in a workbook, they can slow the pace for some students while they increase the challenge for high achievers.

We can not talk about inclusivity without also addressing exclusivity. We would not have to strive to include all students and families if harmful racist and other exclusionary assumptions had not prevented them from being included in the first place. Since these assumptions permeate our society, we must take special care to create an equitable learning environment in our schools. To do this, we must ask ourselves some challenging questions. In her book *Other People's Children: Cultural Conflict in the Classroom*, Lisa D. Delpit, professor at Georgia State University in Atlanta, asks educators if we think of

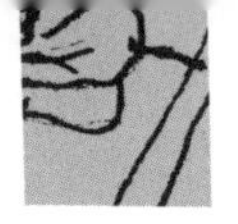

children from varying cultural backgrounds as our own children or as other people's children.[29] If we separate ourselves from certain children, then we may not feel responsible for them. But if we recognize all children as our own, we will ensure that their experiences are honored and that the school reflects and celebrates their perspectives.

Often, respect for other cultures grows out of knowledge and experience. Through learning expeditions that examine cultures in depth, students gain a better understanding of different cultures. Designing multicultural expeditions, however, can be challenging. We may find it hard to locate accurate sources or explore multiple historical perspectives. Cultural stereotypes may limit what we choose to study. For instance, many classes only study Native American art instead of also looking at Lakota zoology or Seminole botany. To avoid these stumbling blocks, we must ask ourselves such difficult questions as "Are stereotypes influencing our work? Are we looking at this culture in a historical vacuum?" To strengthen their own learning experiences, students must also engage in these questions. Expeditionary Learning school designer Kim Archung points out, "Multicultural studies have a tendency to leave out the discourse about racism."[30] When we do this, not only do we perpetuate ignorance, but we also deprive our students of the essential skills of inquiry and critique.

Eloise Biscoe and Wanda Muriel, teachers at Rafael Hernandez School in Boston, Massachusetts, have found that role playing helps students explore

these issues in depth. In a learning expedition about Native American history and culture, they focused on one tribe in a specific historical context. Their fourth-grade students read a novel about the group of Nez Perce who refused to settle on a reservation and were chased by the U.S. Army for 1,200 miles through Idaho and Montana in 1877. The students wrote a play based on the novel and each student took the role of a historical figure. As the students became immersed in the perspective of their characters, they gained a better understanding of the situation, but they also began to break down stereotypes. "They realized that all Native Americans weren't thinking in one unified way and the same was true with the U.S. Army and other government officials," Biscoe explained. "It's hard and it takes time to take another perspective. But it's really important to step into another person's shoes."[31]

The ability to understand other perspectives is becoming more and more essential in our world. As communication, political events, and economic markets become increasingly global, students will need to know how to negotiate within a variety of cultural differences. Not only will the values of diversity and inclusivity help them redress issues of inequality in their own communities, but they will also help them be respectful members of a global community.

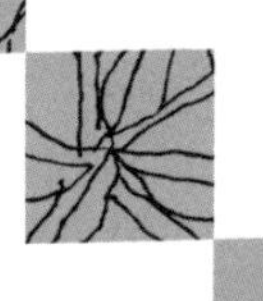

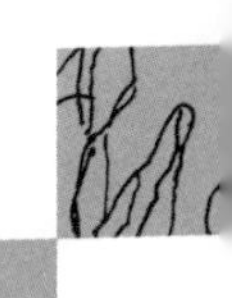

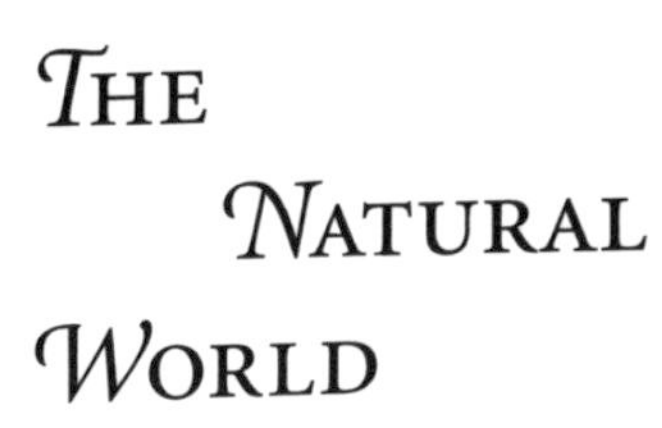

The Natural World

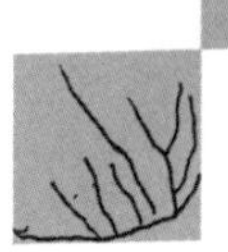

He had missed the deepest of all companionships, a relation with the earth itself, with a countryside and a people. That relationship, he knew, could not be gone after and found; it must be long and deliberate, unconscious.

It must, indeed, be a way of living...and he had begun to believe it the most satisfying tie men can have.

—Willa Cather

Those who dwell... among the beauties and the mysteries of the earth are never alone or weary of life....

Those who contemplate the beauty of the earth find reserves of strength that will endure as long as life lasts.

—Rachel Carson

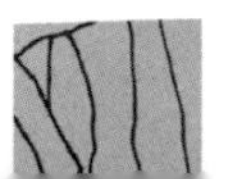

A direct and respectful relationship with the natural world refreshes the human spirit and reveals the important lessons of recurring cycles and cause and effect. Students learn to become stewards of the earth and of the generations to come.

Most school communities consist of teachers, students, parents, and administrators. Expeditionary Learning communities encompass those members, but they also stretch to include the natural world. Instead of tacking "nature studies" on to the end of an afternoon, teachers consistently incorporate the lessons of the natural world into learning expeditions. As students observe life cycles in a classroom garden or take time to reflect in a nearby wooded area, they come to understand that, as humans, they are but one element in a vast, tightly interconnected web. And just as they learn from teachers and parents, they also learn from weather patterns, streams, and peas.

"Now I see the secret of the making of the best persons," Walt Whitman wrote. "It is to grow in the open air, and to eat and sleep with the earth." Indeed, the natural world is an excellent stage upon which students may learn about self-discovery and risk taking. But the landscape itself has its own lessons to teach. Food chains illustrate how life continually changes hands. Forest fires which burn young trees so larger trees can thrive show that nature strikes its own balance. The impact of carbon dioxide on the earth's atmosphere demonstrates the interplay of cause and effect. It is not necessary to have access to tracts of wilderness to explore these cycles. A seed bursting in a jar or ants working in a sand pile offer equal mysteries to investigate.

As students become more familiar with the workings of the natural world, they can begin to cultivate certain habits of interaction. Attentiveness, for instance, is an essential tool for learning about natural processes. Tatanga Mani, a Stoney Indian from Canada, once asked "Did you know that trees talk? Well they do. They talk to each other and they'll talk to you if you listen." Listening, though, is an art that has to be practiced. In a learning expedition entitled "Natural Reflections" at Central Alternative High School in Dubuque, Iowa, students learned to listen and see. Teacher Katherine Stevens asked the students to keep a daily journal charting the development of a tree from March to June. At first, paying such close attention to one tree seemed like a waste of time to her students. Yet as they started to focus on the tree—to really see it—endless details and changes popped out at them. Their first drawings, with arrow-straight branches and cloudlike leaves, represented an idea of a tree. Later in the year, the drawings took on the exactitude that comes from close observation.

The act of observation drew the students into a relationship with the trees, and from that grew the habits of respect and admiration. One of Stevens' students was particularly impressed with the way a tree could grow out of a sandstone bluff. "He would write about lying on his stomach across the large rock and wondering how this tiny tree, only 21 inches tall—he measured it twice—could grow out of this rock," Stevens said.[32] At the end of the year, the student moved away from Dubuque, but before he left, he climbed the steep bluff with two friends so he could show them his special tree.

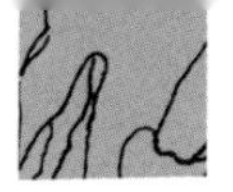

Coming to appreciate a nonhuman being helps remind us that we share our environment with countless other living things. Since we share this planet, we must do our part in maintaining its health. The more students learn about the natural world, the more they realize the importance of becoming stewards of the earth. Learning expeditions foster stewardship by asking students to apply what they learn in their own communities. For instance, Shutesbury Elementary School in Shutesbury, Massachusetts, embarked on a whole school, yearlong learning expedition on water. After studying watersheds, the geology of local waterways, and aquatic populations, the students embarked on the town's first testing of private wells for lead and sodium pollution.

This project had serious consequences. Since nearby towns had discovered dangerous levels of lead and sodium, the community anxiously awaited the students' findings. If there was pollution, treatment plans would have to be devised; property values might decline. Local newspapers tracked the students' progress, while members of the Board of Health asked to be included in their study. These high stakes inspired the students to collect their samples and analyze their data with utmost care. They checked and double checked. Finally, the students announced that lead and sodium levels were acceptable throughout town, although lead levels were higher in wells where the water was more acidic. Having learned for themselves what sustains healthy aquifers, the students went on to ensure that the whole community had access to toxin-free water.

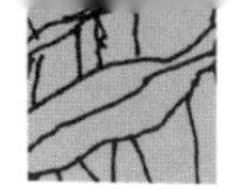

While the natural world is teeming with lessons about cycles and stewardship, it also offers one of our most replenishing retreats. Humans are never alone in nature, but finding a quiet spot can soothe a harried soul or inspire unexpected insights. When we bring with us the habits of attentiveness and respect, all sorts of beauty and detail become clear to us. A first-grade student at the Rocky Mountain School of Expeditionary Learning wrote about a few of the wonders she noticed when conducting fieldwork in a forest outside of Denver. "I like the way the snow sparkles and the sound your shoes make on the snow and the feel of the wind blowing against my back. You can also see lots of tracks."[33]

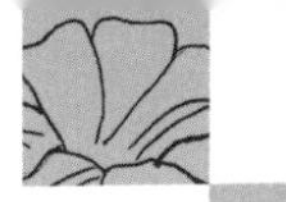

Solitude and Reflection

I like it when they make us reflect on what we did. It makes you look back and say, "Oh, I can do this better next time." You can reflect on anything after you do it, and it makes you feel like you studied all night for a final exam and you really feel good about it.

You feel more experienced when you look back on things and figure out how to make them better.

—Rory Murray, Sixth Grader
Rafael Hernandez School,
Boston, Massachusetts.

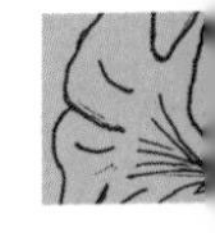

Silence was meaningful with the Lakota, and his granting a space of silence to the speech-maker and his own moment of silence before talking was done in the practice of true politeness and regard for the rule that,

"thought comes before speech."

—Luther Standing Bear
(Oglala Lakota)

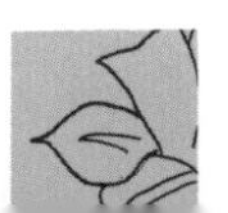

Solitude, reflection, and silence replenish our energies and open our minds.

Be sure students have time alone to explore their own thoughts, make their own connections, and create their own ideas.

Then give them opportunity to exchange their reflections with each other and with adults.

Teachers and learners the world over understand that the stillness of solitude reaps vibrant benefits. "I don't retreat from the world to escape," Robert Frost said, "but to return stronger." Solitude is cocoon time. It helps develop powers of concentration and allows thoughts to gestate and new realizations to surface. Scientists and artists alike attest to the "click," the unanticipated connections they make when constructively immersed in solitude. The same process occurs for students. Not only do periods of reflection refresh their nervous systems, but they also allow students to ask questions about themselves, examine their inner lives, and discover their own springs of growth and self-renewal. Our schools—and hence our professional development as well—offer people the time and space to plumb these depths and replenish their energy for learning.

Despite their numerous benefits, periods of solitude and reflection are virtually unknown in public schools today. It might seem impossible to create solitude in the midst of bustling activity, but it is actually quite easy. It costs no extra money or resources; it requires only silence, commitment, and an imaginative use of existing time and space. Many Expeditionary Learning schools make room for solitude by reserving ten or twenty minutes a day for silent reflection time. In some schools, part of the community circle is set aside for students to close their eyes and gain solitude. In other schools, students find a comfortable spot in the classroom to read quietly, or to sit and think.

While quiet reflection is an individual process, it also has the ability to strengthen community ties. People often return from quiet reflection or solitude with a renewed appreciation for the people around them. Expeditionary Learning schools experience this paradoxical process. For instance, Mark Weiss, the principal of School for the Physical City in New York City, believes that the five minutes of silence his school shares at their daily community meeting has enhanced their sense of togetherness. "I think there is a feeling that the silence is part of our culture," he says. "We are proud of a school that can be quiet for five minutes in the course of a hectic New York City day."[34] Though each student sits alone with his or her own thoughts, together they set a tone of purposefulness and depth for the entire school day.

In addition to fostering renewal, solitude and reflection bolster academic learning. David Kolb, the Harvard psychologist, suggested that learning requires time set aside explicitly for reflecting on experience.[35] If learners are not encouraged to reflect, they will be less likely to derive lessons that redirect and build on their understandings. Expeditionary Learning teachers honor this step in the learning process by incorporating journal writing and silent time into the school day, but these tools are especially useful in helping students build knowledge and understanding from their fieldwork experiences.

Journal writing, for instance, helped first-grade students from Rocky Mountain School of

Expeditionary Learning make sense of their fieldwork in Castlewood Canyon outside of Denver. On their first trip to study the canyon's natural history and the broken dam that caused a terrible flood in 1933, the students garnered general impressions and cursory observations. But each time they went back they noticed more. Their teacher, Peter Thulson, encouraged them to write in their journals about what they saw. Soon they began to write about animal tracks in the snow, interesting plants, and heron feathers lying below a rookery. They began to postulate about the strange looking remnants of a dam. Was it an old castle ruined in a war? Were they in the midst of building a new building? These journal entries became the foundation of their understanding of the canyon. They also helped the students write an in-depth guidebook so future visitors could discover the canyon for themselves.

In a similar way, teachers also benefit from reflecting on their experiences. They too notice more and gain new insights when they pause and think about their practice and their work with colleagues. Many Expeditionary Learning schools schedule "Reflection Days," so teachers can look back on recent expeditions, celebrate successes, and get feedback from colleagues on how to improve in the future. At Douglass Intermediate School in San Antonio, Texas, principal Elida Bera and instructional guide Becky Bordelon redesigned the faculty's lesson plans to mirror the school's commitment to reflection. Now in addition to listing the week's plans, teachers also reflect

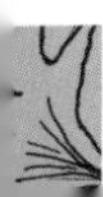

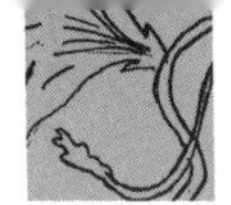

on the process of planning and guiding the learning expedition. One teacher wrote, "I wish I could get more of my plans completed. So I ask myself 'What can I do to improve this?' I am going to stick closer to my schedule. I must get help with pacing." By putting such structures in place, Expeditionary Learning honors the role reflection plays in growth.

As we become increasingly bombarded with background noise and visual images, periods of silence and reflection take on greater significance. Sitting alone in a grove of trees or writing in a journal can provide much needed islands of renewal and thoughtfulness. Teachers and students alike may find this process awkward in the beginning, yet the fruits of their labor will inspire them to continue. As one teacher wrote of a solo experience on an Outward Bound wilderness course, "The solitude was difficult at first, but in the end it was like loosening a knot. All sorts of thoughts, feelings, observations were allowed to pass through." When this process becomes a daily activity, students and teachers tap stores of creative potential.

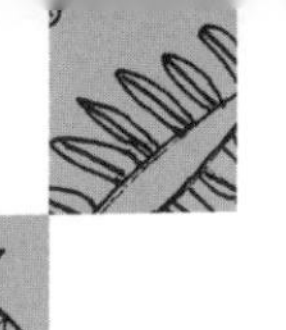

Service and Compassion

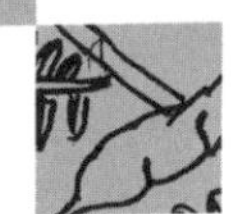

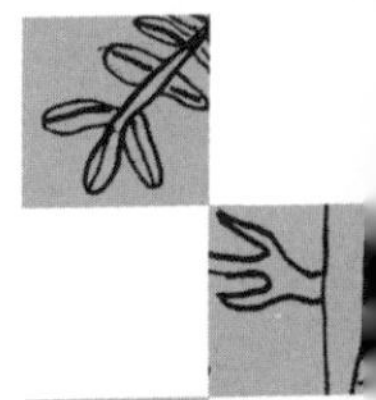

It is not the brains that matter most, but that which guides them—the character, the heart, generous qualities, progressive ideas.

—Fyodor Dostoyevski

The ultimate measure of a man is not where he stands in moments of comfort and conveniences, but where he stands in times of challenge and controversy.

—Martin Luther King, Jr.

We are crew, not passengers, and are strengthened by acts of consequential service to others.

One of a school's primary functions is to prepare its students with the attitudes and skills to learn from and be of service to others.

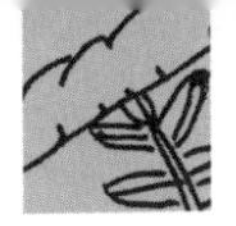

Kurt Hahn said, "You can preach at [students]; that is the hook without the worm. You can order them to volunteer; that is of the devil. You can say to them, 'You are needed,' and that appeal hardly ever fails." Countless studies have confirmed Hahn's belief that students solve problems and surpass expectations when they know their work will benefit others. To tap this potential, Expeditionary Learning integrates sustained, consequential service into learning expeditions. These ongoing projects represent the connection of intellectual and character development, for not only do students learn the skills necessary to solve real-world problems, but they also develop the habit of being active and compassionate community members.

A rich body of research and theory has demonstrated that service, when properly structured, can have a powerful impact on young people's intellectual development. Many researchers have demonstrated the dislocation between learning that occurs in out-of-school settings, or practical intelligence, and that which goes on in school, or school-related intelligence. This growing body of research confirms what thoughtful teachers have known all along: the most powerful kinds of learning experiences happen when knowing and doing are bound together; that is, when abstract concepts are taught in the context of situations where their meaning and real-world applications are apparent.

Service helps young people see this connection between academic content and the problems

people encounter in everyday life. It provides an opportunity to test and apply knowledge they have gained beyond the settings in which the learning occurred. When middle school students at Rafael Hernandez School in Boston, Massachusetts, participated in an architecture expedition, they did not just plan dream houses. Instead, they designed ways to transform a nearby vacant lot into a community space. They had learned in their studies that urban design projects work best when they address community needs, so they surveyed hundreds of community members. They then used their skills of building architectural, scale models to design the community center, park, and gardens requested by the community.

When students enter the arena of real-world problems, they confront real-world challenges and expectations. The Hernandez students had to go to City Hall to research zoning ordinances and to the Harvard Graduate School of Design to discuss scale models with architects. Meeting professional standards deepened student learning. As a number of researchers have found, problem-solving abilities increase for students who are involved in community service groups more than for comparable children who are not, because students are more willing to grapple with problems when they know the outcome will have an impact on their community.[36] Their efforts often receive rewards that mean far more than letter grades. When Boston commissioned urban planners to generate designs for the vacant lot near Hernandez School, the planners began by consulting with the students. Planner Greg Murphy explained, "We wanted to acknowledge that what they did was work that professionals do out in the world. We wanted them to know that people value what they did."[37]

Bridging the gap between in-and out-of-school learning is essential. But equally important are the social development outcomes of service for students. Service has been shown to improve young people's sense of social and personal responsibility, and attitudes toward adults and others. But as Diane Hedin has written, "If the objective is real change in the way that young people view their obligation to the community, it cannot be assumed that the young person is the primary beneficiary of the service. Youth service is powerful because it benefits the community as much as it does the student."[38]

Expeditionary Learning encourages students to discern what projects will offer authentic service to the community. Not only does this sharpen their abilities to assess social responsibility, but it also intensifies the students' level of commitment. A representative from the Portland Housing Authority asked fourth graders at Jack Elementary School in Portland, Maine, what would help the housing project where many of them lived. One student observed that most children in the project ride bikes but can not afford to fix them. "I think we should have a bike shop," he said. "Kids need a cheap place to get their bikes fixed."[39] Thus was born the Kids' Quick Fix Bike Shop in which students repaired bikes, provided safety lessons, and adjusted prices so all could afford their services. Knowing that

children would benefit from their work, the students were more than willing to apply for grants, consult safety experts, interview mechanics, and handle the accounting of the shop. When the shop opened, the neighborhood children gained a service they needed, while the Jack students gained a sense of empowerment. "There has been a great difference in their self-esteem, and the way they feel about themselves," teacher Karen White says. "I really feel like they believe there is nothing they can't do."[40]

By placing service at the heart of learning expeditions, Expeditionary Learning schools encourage students to see service not as an isolated action, but as a way of being a member of a community. Students turn from society's growing sense of fragmentation and focus on their responsibility to the whole. They learn to generate constructive responses to community needs. One student arrived at this definition of activism: "When you're in a situation and normally you would react in the same way as everyone else, even though you know it's wrong, instead you do or say something different, something that will change it."[41]

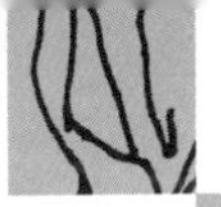

Notes

[1] Eric Copage, ed., *Black Pearls* (New York: William Morrow, 1993), March 23.

[2] Loretta Brady and Denis Udall, "Can We Change the World?" in *Fieldwork, Volume II*, Amy Mednick and Emily Cousins, eds. (Dubuque, IA: Kendall/Hunt, 1996), p. 47.

[3]Learning expeditions are a form of curriculum, instruction, and assessment through which teachers and students pursue long-term intellectual investigations built around significant projects and performances. The investigations take students out into the world, bring the world into the classroom, and often provide students with opportunities to serve the wider community. Learning expeditions focus on critical thinking, essential skills and habits, and character development. Ongoing assessment is woven throughout the expeditions, pushing students to higher levels of performance. For in-depth examples of learning expeditions, see *Journeys through our Classrooms,* Denis Udall and Amy Mednick eds. (Dubuque, IA: Kendall/Hunt, 1996).

[4] Leah Rugen, "Joining Intellectual and Character Development: An Impossible Task?" *in Fieldwork, Volume II*, p. 35.

[5] Ron Berger, "Stream Day One," in *The Web*, vol. III, no. 8, October, 1995, p. 5.

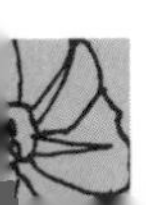

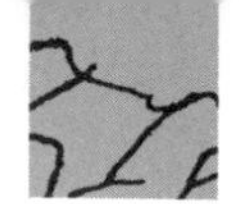

[6] Eleanor Duckworth, *The Having of Wonderful Ideas* (New York: Teachers College Press, 1987), p. 14.

[7] Donna Green, Larry Wheeler, John Sweeney, et. al., "Where in the World are We? The Physics of Location," in *Journeys through our Classrooms*, p. 109.

[8] Lorie Duclos and Meg Campbell, "When Teachers Change," in *The Web*, vol. V, no. 5, May, 1997, p. 5.

[9] Green, Wheeler, Sweeney, et. al., p. 111.

[10] Ibid., p. 113.

[11] Vivian Stephens, "Learning Noise," in *Journeys through our Classrooms*, p. 72.

[12] Mary Lynn Lewark, "Let's Practice: Revision in a First-Grade Classroom," in *Journeys through our Classrooms,* p. 19.

[13] Kathy Greeley, "Making Theater, Making Sense," in *Journeys through our Classrooms,* p. 50.

[14] Tammy Duehr & Shari Flatt with Emily Cousins, "Truck, Boat, Train, Bus: A First-Grade Expedition into Transportation," in *Journeys through our Classrooms,* p. 135.

[15] Ibid., p. 135.

[16] Chris Weaver, "Intimacy, Class Size, and Taffy the Chicken," in *The Web*, vol. V, no. 7, October, 1997, p. 1.

[17] Ibid, p. 1.

[18] Stephens, p. 71.

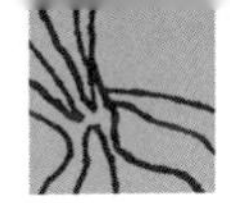

[19] Magda Rodriguez and Amy Mednick, "In the Spotlight: A Conversation with Magda Rodriguez," in *The Web,* vol. V, no. 4, April, 1997, p. 4.

[20] Ron Berger, "Stream Day One," in *Fieldwork, Volume II*, p. 123.

[21] Thomas James, "The Only Mountain Worth Climbing: An Historical and Philosophical Exploration of Outward Bound and Its Link to Education," in *Fieldwork, Volume I,* Emily Cousins and Melissa Rodgers, eds. (Dubuque, IA: Kendall/ Hunt, 1995), p. 60.

[22] Kathy Greeley and Amy Mednick, "Leaving the Ledge," in *Fieldwork, Volume II*, p. 92.

[23] Berger, 1996, p. 124.

[24] "Maxine Greene on Leadership: An Interview," in *Klingenstein Newsletter* (Winter, 1990) vol. I.

[25] Joseph Newkirk, "Students Designing for Students: The Minisink Expedition," in *Fieldwork, Volume II,* p. 45.

[26] Green, Wheeler, Sweeney, et. al., p. 114.

[27] Mieko Kamii, "Practitioners Discuss Portfolios: Your Best Work is What's Expected of You," in *Fieldwork, Volume II*, p. 71-73.

[28] Mieko Kamii, "Having Wonderful Ideas: An Interview with Eleanor Duckworth," *in Fieldwork, Volume I*, p. 72.

[29] Lisa Delpit, *Other People's Children: Cultural Conflict in the Classroom* (New York: The New Press, 1995).

[30] Kim Archung, "Diversity and Inclusivity: A Closer Look at Multicultural Curricula," in *Fieldwork, Volume II*, p. 138.

[31] "Teaching and Learning in a Diverse Cultural Setting," in *The Web*, vol. V, no. 6, September, 1997, p. 11.

[32] Katherine Stevens, "Natural Reflections," in *Fieldwork, Volume II*, p. 32.

[33] Peter Thulson, "Looking, and Looking Again," in *The Web*, vol. IV, no. 6, June, 1996, p. 7.

[34] "A Conversation with Expeditionary Learning Principals," in *Fieldwork, Volume I*, p. 112.

[35] David Kolb, *Experiential Learning: Experience as the Source of Learning and Development* (Englewood Cliffs, NJ: Prentice Hall, 1984).

[36] See, for instance, Diane Hedin, "The Power of Community Service," *in Proceedings of The Academy of Political Science*, Vol. 37, No. 2, 1989.

[37] Emily Cousins, "Service: Crew, Not Passengers," in Fieldwork, *Volume I*, p. 127.

[38] Diane Hedin, "The Power of Community Service in Caring for America's Children," in *The Academy of Political Science*, Frank Macciarera and Alan Gartner eds., 37(2).

[39] Cousins, p. 127.

[40] Ibid., p. 129.

[41] Connie Russell-Rodriguez and April Cotte, "Urban Exploration: Making a Difference," in *Fieldwork Volume II*, p. 41.

Acknowledgments

We thank the Dubuque, Iowa students whose artwork illustrates *Reflections on Design Principles*: Alicia Brokus, Theresa Kurtz, Amber Waddick, Mark Mitchley, Emilee Clark, and Shayna Nesteby from Bryant Elementary School; and Stephanie Thielen, Michael Mangers, Krista Ansel, Megan Kalmes, and Josh Fee from Table Mound Elementary School.

About the Author: Emily Cousins is the service director of Expeditionary Learning Outward Bound. She has worked with the organization since its inception in 1992. A writer and editor, Cousins lives in Missoula, Montana.

Book cover and interior pages designed by Carroll Conquest, Conquest Design.

Outward Bound USA
Route 9D, R2 Box 280
Garrison, NY 10524-9757
(914) 424-4000

Expeditionary Learning Outward Bound
122 Mount Auburn St.
Cambridge, MA 02138
(617) 576-1260
info@elob.org